Ansar Beit al-Maqdis

Sinai

A Russian civilian plane with 217 passengers and 7 crew aboard crashed over Sinai early Saturday morning, Oct. 31, shortly after taking off from the Sinai resort town of Sharm el-Sheikh for St. Petersburg.

Initial reporting on the fate of the plane was confused and is still not completely clear. It was first reported to be missing after contact was lost with Egyptian air control; it was then said to be safely on its way to Russia over Turkey. Russian aviation sources then reported the A321 to be missing over Cypriot air space. Finally, the Egyptian prime minister's office Egyptian prime minister's office confirmed that a Russian passenger plane had crashed in central Sinai and a cabinet level crisis committee had been formed to deal with the crash.

The airliner owned by the small airline Kogalymavia disappeared from screen 23 minutes after takeoff from Sharm el-Sheikh. There were many families with children aboard.

The first claim by Russian aviation sources that the plane had gone missing over Cyprus was an attempt to draw attention from the likelihood that it was shot down over Sinai, where the former Ansar al-Maqdis, which has renamed itself ISIS-Sinai, maintains its main strongholds.

On board the plane were 17 children, along with 200 adults and seven crew, said aviation authorities. There are no signs of survivors. Confirming the deliberate attempt at confusion, Moscow and Cairo both stated that the plane had disappeared from the radar 23 minutes after takeoff from Sharm El-Sheikh.

This is refuted by the discovery of the wreckage, a few minutes ago, completely gutted and destroyed, and a short distance away near Bir Al-Hassaneh, in the central Sinai Jabal al-Halal mountain range, where Ansar Beit al-Miqdas terrorists are holed up and which is almost inaccessible to rescue teams.

It is to this stronghold that ISIS sent officers, former senior members of Saddam Hussein's army, to set up a major campaign against the Egyptian army, along with advanced anti-air missile systems smuggled into Sinai and the Gaza Strip from Libya for this campaign.

In another attempt to disguise the cause of the disaster, Russian and Egyptian officials now say that the pilot of the Russian plane reported a technical fault after takeoff and asked to be rerouted to Cairo or El-Arish. Russian and Egyptian officials have meanwhile announced they are forming commissions of inquiry to investigate the cause of the tragedy. Official condolences were relayed to the waiting families the airport.

The Sinai branch of the Islamic State has developed a highly competent intelligence-gathering network operated by local Bedouin tribesmen who track the slightest movements in the Peninsula. The Egyptian army and the American troops serving at the big the Multinational Force base there are fully aware of the round-the-clock surveillance maintained by the terrorists at Egyptian resorts, using staff at hotels, restaurants and the local airfield as inside informers.

Ansar has never yet harmed the tourist traffic in Sinai. But once ISIS decided to use it to hit back at Russia's intensified military intervention in the Syrian conflict, the Islamists would not have found it hard to find out when the Russian airliner was due to take off from the Red Sea resort, chart its route north along the western coast of the Gulf of Aqaba up to Dahab and then turn west towards central Sinai and head for the Mediterranean. All the terrorists had to do was to lay a missile ambush for the plane from the Jabal Halal eminence of 876 meters (2,865 ft).

Russian sources following the forensic examination of the bodies and partial remains of the victims flown to St. Petersburg report that they show evidence of an explosion in the plane before it plummeted to the ground. Further testing is required to establish the cause of the explosion.

A US infrared satellite detected a heat flash at the same time and same vicinity over Sinai where the Russian plane went down. A US defense official added that the same satellite would have been able to track the tell-tale heat trail of a missile from the ground. "The speculation that this plane was brought down by a missile is off the table," the official said.

Another official said, "the plane disintegrated at a very high altitude." The general consensus ahead of the Egyptian and Russian probes is that a sudden, catastrophic explosion caused the crash - whether from a bomb inside, "external impact" — as the Metrojet company claims - or from faulty fuel. Russian fuel experts found nothing wrong with the fuel.

An Egyptian physician who inspected the scene of the disaster found that one out of every five bodies he saw had been incinerated to death from a fire that may have started in the passenger's cabin and spread to the rest of the plane. Egyptian experts reported that "the large number of separate body fragments" could indicate that a strong explosion occurred onboard before the aircraft hit the ground. They were scattered across a radius of 8-10 square kilometers from the wreckage.

Russian and Egyptian sources tracking the examination of the two black boxes found evidence that the calamity occurred too rapidly for the pilots or crew to send an SOS or even say a few words.

As the probe of the air catastrophe began Tuesday and Wednesday, Moscow and Cairo were increasingly at odds on their findings. The Russians asserted that the plane must have broken up into two parts as a result of a strong explosion, whereas Egyptian officials remained intent on playing down the claim of responsibility for the crash published Saturday by the Sinai wing of the Islamic State. They criticize the Russians as rushing to conclusions ahead of the probe.

Egyptian President Abdel-Fatteh El-Sisi arrived in London Wednesday for talks with British Prime Minister David Cameron. In interviews prior to his arrival, the Egyptian president said that he will demand that David Cameron "complete his mission in Libya to prevent the country being dominated by Islamists."By "mission," El-Sisi was referring to the UK's role in the coalition which toppled Muammar Qaddafi in 2011.

Egypt faces an acute problem from Libya's transformation in the last two years into the main supply source of smuggled arms and fighters for the Islamist terrorists operating in Egypt and Sinai.While neither the Egyptians or the Russians are willing to admit this, it is highly likely that the missile or explosives which brought down the Russian airliner Saturday came from Libya.

Press release

"The fighters of the Islamic State were able to down a Russian plane over Sinai province that was carrying over 220 Russian crusaders. They were all killed, thanks be to God," said a statement from the Sinai affiliate of ISIS

The terrorists' statement went on to say: *"You should know, Russians and your allies, that you have no security on Muslim land or its airspace… The daily murder of scores of innocents in Syria by your air bombardments will bring upon you disasters… Just as you kill, so you will be killed…"* |

In an audio recording release via social networks, ISIS repeated its claim of responsibility for the downing of a Russian airliner over the Sinai Peninsula on Saturday, adding that it will soon reveal how it shot down the jet. The message also challenged the government of Egypt to prove that ISIS was not responsible for the crash.

Britain has canceled flights indefinitely to and from Sharm el-Sheikh due to security concerns after the downing of the Russian airliner, leaving 20,000 British holidaymakers stranded there. Downing Street has cited an explosive device as the possible cause of the Russian jet's crash over Sinai killing all 224 people aboard. PM David Cameron has called a second Cobra (emergency cabinet) meeting to review the situation ahead of his lunch date with visiting Egyptian president Abdel-Fatteh El-Sisi. Foreign Secretary Philip Hammond says that plans are in place to evacuate the tourists.

Background

Ansar Beit al-Maqdis (ABM), also known as the Sinai Province, is a Salafi jihadist group that formed in Egypt and the Gaza Strip in 2011. After authoritarian president Hosni Mubarak was ousted from power in Egypt in 2011, tribal communities in Sinai, which claimed that they were oppressed by the Egyptian government, drove security forces out of the region. In this power vacuum, members of the region's active militant population joined the militant group Al-Tawhidwa'al-Jihad to merge and form ABM.

ABM shares a similar ideology as Al Qaeda (AQ) and declared themselves AQ's wing in the Sinai in 2011. However, despite sharing similar ideology, ABM and AQ were never formal affiliates. Since its formation, judged to be at some point in 2011, the group seems to have gained support in the peninsula, seeming to breathe life into jihadi cells that had been neutralized by former campaigns in the Sinai.

This has been evidenced by the leadership of the group, many of whom are experienced militants who had previously been allied with other jihadi groups, particularly Tawhidwal-Jihad and the MujahideenShura Council (MSC) in the Environs of Jerusalem.

The group ingratiates itself to local population, calling on them to stand with Ansar Bayt al-Maqdis in their fight against the state. In a recent campaign, the group had been reported to be distributing fliers to local (and highly marginalized) populations that stated: "If you are not with us, do not be against us." In a recent statement, the group described itself as "your brothers…men from [Egypt]…perhaps your neighbors or relatives."

According to intelligence reports, the group is thought to have around 1,000 members, many of whom may have operated in other jihadi groups in the past. This number, however, is difficult to verify given the group's refusal to speak with members of the international press and the many reports of alleged killings or arrest of members from the Egyptian army.

Regardless of exact numbers, the group is known to be the strongest and best coordinated in Egypt, and it is in possession of advanced weaponry, including man-portable air-defense systems (MANPADS), rocket-propelled grenades, Grad rockets, and mortars. Additionally, since swearing Bay'a (an oath of allegiance) to the Islamic State on November 10, 2014, there has been a dramatic advance in the group's media capabilities and production, as well as an overall re-branding that showcases the strong tie to the greater Islamic State.

Egyptian security forces have launched a number of successful operations against Ansar Bayt al-Maqdis operatives, including a March 2014 raid that resulted in the death of six militants, the capture of eight others, and yielded a cache of weapons and strategic documents.

On April 9, 2014, the United States declared Ansar Bayt al-Maqdis a terrorist organization. Egypt followed suit shortly thereafter, declaring the group to be a terrorist organization on April 14, 2014.

Ansar Bayt al-Maqdis released a statement on July 25, 2014, lamenting the death of three of its leaders by an "Israeli drone;" Egyptian authorities vehemently denied the penetration of airspace. Despite these setbacks, the group continues to be active in the Sinai, releasing regular and frequent statements on social media.

On November 10, 2014, Ansar Bayt al-Maqdis formally swore allegiance (Bay'a) to the Islamic State, changing their name to Wilayat Sinai (Province of Sinai) which is the most significant, and potentially long-lasting recent development for the group. This allegiance provides the Islamic State with a "province" in Sinai, an extension of territory for their overall Caliphate, while also providing Ansar Bayt al-Maqdis with greater resources.

These resources are apparent when examining the increase in production value of Ansar Bayt al-Maqdis' media releases, that the Islamic State puts heavy focus upon, and also in the increased legitimacy and support the group receives from abroad. Evidence toward this point can be found in the media released statement calling for foreign fighters to travel to the Sinai to help solidify the Caliphate.

Attacks

Early statements from the Ansar Bayt al-Maqdis mainly targeted the Jewish population in nearby Israel, where the majority of the group's efforts were focused (with the exception of pipeline attacks on Egyptian soil).

Soon after the removal of President Muhammed Morsi, however, Ansar Bayt al-Maqdis shifted its attention to the Egyptian government for waging war against Islam. Since aligning themselves with the Islamic State, the group has adopted some, but not all of the Islamic State's ideology. The act of beheading enemies, especially those they deem as traitors has become more frequent since the group pledged themselves to the Islamic State, showing a clear evolution of their practices.

Despite claiming responsibility for the killing of American oil worker William Henderson, there is little evidence that Ansar Bayt al-Maqdis holds the intense anti-Western and sectarian ideologies of the Islamic State as a priority; the group's focus remains on Egyptian security forces.

Ansar Bayt al-Maqdis has attacked gas pipelines and a tourist bus in its efforts to wage economic war. The group has claimed responsibility for several pipeline attacks, as far back as February 5, 2011, and as late as January 17, 2014. In a highly coordinated attack on August 18, 2011, the group attacked a bus in Eilat, Israel, killing at least eight Israelis and three Egyptian security forces.

In its first attack after the ouster of President Muhammad Morsi, on September 5, 2013Ansar Bayt al-Maqdis attempted to assassinate Minister of the Interior, Mohamed Ibrahim, but was unsuccessful. This attack was carried out by former Egyptian military officer WalidBadr, who had traveled to wage jihad in Syria, was also known to have connections with the Muhammad Jamal Network.

The group's deadliest known attack to date was a December 24, 2013 attack on the Security Directorate building in Mansoura. This remains one of the deadliest attacks in Egypt in the past decade: 16 people were killed and 134 were injured in the bombing. This bombing also represented a moment of intense escalation in the Egyptian government's "war on terror;" despite not having been connected with the attack, the Muslim Brotherhood was declared a terrorist group the following day.

Also on the day after the Mansoura attack, Ansar Bayt al-Maqdis released a video of an attack on a helicopter. Militants used a man-portable air-defense system (MANPADS) to take down the aircraft, killing the five men on board.

In its first attack on tourists, an Ansar Bayt al-Maqdis suicide bomber attacked a bus of South Korean tourists traveling near the Israeli border on February 16, 2014. The attack killed three of the tourists and the Egyptian bus driver.

The group was engaged in a campaign against Israel during a period of the intense conflict between Israel and Gaza in July 2014. The group released videos of Grad and 107mm rocket attacks on the Israeli town of Eilat, two attacks on the village BneiNetzarim, and an attack on an Israeli border military base.

In August, 2014, Ansar Bayt al-Maqdis turned its attention back to Egypt. The group released a video first documenting the murder of Egyptian police on August 18. Ten days later, on August 28, the group released a video in which they document the beheading of four Egyptian men they accuse of collaboration with Israeli intelligence. The August beheadings were the first violence of this type for the group, marking a chilling change in tactic that has endured through the posting of this profile in February 2015.

On October 24, 2014, Ansar Bayt al-Maqdis carried out what was its deadliest attack up until that point. The group detonated a car bomb at a heavily guarded security checkpoint in Sheikh Zuweid and then ambushed the guards who came to investigate the attack. Later the same day, they opened fire on a security checkpoint in Al-Arish. The attacks killed at least 33 Egyptian security forces and wounded as many. This was the at that point deadliest attack on the Egyptian military in decades.

On January 29, 2015, Ansar Bayt al-Maqdis carried out an attack reminiscent of their earlier October strike against the military. The group utilized suicide bombers, car bombs, mortars, and intense gunfire against a military base and nearby security buildings, a hotel, a police club, a newspaper office, and various security checkpoints through North Sinai. The result was over 30 dead Egyptian military members and many more wounded.

The scale and immense coordination of the attacks, along with the general escalation of their ability to strike at military targets points toward the group's overall cohesion. It might also point toward evidence that the widespread military crackdown on militants in the Sinai by the Egyptian military may not be experiencing the success that the military claim it has.

Ansar Bayt al-Maqdis has planted 21 bombs almost daily along several routes taken by the army and security officials in north Sinai in the areas stretching from el-Arish to Rafah and Sheikh Zuweid.

The security apparatus has succeeded in discovering and dismantling seven bombs, while 14 others exploded. Six bombs targeted military vehicles, killing four security men and wounding 24 others, some of whom were in critical condition, mostly soldiers and officers. Eight bombs exploded without hitting their target.

Ansar Bayt al-Maqdis is increasingly using bombs because they are unable to face the Egyptian army, which is better equipped and larger. As a result, the army outdoes them in direct confrontations, which it is well trained for.

Ansar Bayt al-Maqdis has lately succeeded in opening fronts inside other Egyptian districts, especially after pledging allegiance to IS. Several people who had always dreamed of the jihadist caliphate joined the group, in addition to defecting members from the Muslim Brotherhood, notably those holding a grudge against the state due to the Rabia and al-Nahda massacres.

In the evening of Friday, Nov. 28, Ansar Bayt al-Maqdis — or Wilayat Sinai as it is now called — claimed responsibility for the assassination of a colonel and two soldiers from the Egyptian army in the Suez bridge area in the heart of Cairo, and the killing of an officer and a soldier in Qalyubia governorate. The group declared in an online statement that the two attacks were carried out by a brigade affiliated to it and called the Martyr AbiUbaidah al-Masri Brigade.

All the latest terrorist operations carried out by Ansar Bayt al-Maqdis confirm that the group relies on the remote targeting strategy in booby-trapping operations, assassinations or bombing of vital state infrastructure such as gas pipelines. This also confirms that the organization is avoiding direct confrontation with the Egyptian army, fearing the loss of its few members, according to sources close to the organization. Moreover, activists and observers in Sinai fear the increase in members of terrorist organizations in the future, if the state continues to fight terrorism with foul practices that harm civilians in the peninsula.

Regarding the bombing of the gas pipelines in Sinai, the jihadist source said that Ansar Bayt al-Maqdis will keep bombing gas pipelines for three reasons. First, the organization wants to regain its media momentum to prove that it is facing the tough military campaigns in Sinai. Second, it wants to cause losses to the army's economic structure — a structure that greatly relies on the huge profits from cement factories in the center of Sinai and uses gas in its work. Third, the organization wants to stop pumping gas exported to Jordan because the latter joined the anti-IS international alliance.

The Egyptian army's cement plants and other plants owned by businessmen close to the ruling regime in Cairo are suffering losses due to the suspension of production, which is described by one of the workers in these plants as a disaster. Meanwhile, the state is also suffering substantial losses. An officer at the Egyptian Natural Gas Co. (Gasco), the main operator in charge of gas repairs in Sinai, told that every time a pipeline is blown up, the repairs cost millions of Egyptian pounds paid from the state budget.

The Gasco source said that the losses also affected Jordan, which depends on Egyptian gas to generate electricity, stressing that it is impossible to secure the gas lines that are exposed and stretch over 100 kilometers (62 miles) in the vast desert. *"This violates the economic contracts signed with Jordan and exposes the two countries to significant economic losses,"* he said.

One of the managers at the Sinai cement factory, in the industrial zone affected by the gas explosions in central Sinai, told *"The citizens will incur the consequences of the losses and terrorist operations, including the bombing of the gas pipeline."*

"The repeated bombings prompted the departments in charge of the operation of the plants — whether private or military plants — to raise the sale price by 25% as a result of the increase in the production cost. This increase came in response to attempts to replace gas with diesel, which is more costly, especially in terms of transportation to central Sinai," he added.

It is noteworthy that el-Arish's gas pipeline has been bombed 25 times since the regime of former President Hosni Mubarak was toppled.

All information and analyses from the field indicate that the coming phase will be very tough for Egypt, with the potential shift of violence from Sinai to the core of Egypt.

In a recent article published on the website Minbar al Tawhidwa'l Jihad, leading global jihad ideologue Sheikh Abu al Mundhir al Shinqiti called on Egypt's Muslims to wage jihad against Egyptian security forces, in particular within the Sinai Peninsula. According to Shinqiti, the Egyptian army *"is an army of infidels and apostates"* that is no different from the armies of the US, Israel, or the regime of Bashar al Assad in Syria.

"[B]elonging to this army is apostasy from Islam and a pledge of allegiance to the enemies of Allah. Belonging to this army is belonging to a sect that is at war with Allah," Shinqiti wrote. He further argued that *"Muslim women married to a member of the army should know that their marriage is nullified because [their husbands] are apostates."*

In the article, al Shinqiti also questioned the Muslim Brotherhood's approach to the July 2013 overthrow of Mohammed Morsi. Shinqiti also declared that anyone advocating non-violence *"is a criminal thug who wants the Ummah to be eradicated and to be slaughtered."*

According to Shinqiti, the Egyptian army must be fought as *"peaceful change … is now impossible."* *"Every attempt to avoid fighting the Egyptian Army is like treating a disease with the wrong medicine,"* he wrote. Shinqiti further called on Egyptian Muslims to *"come and respond to the call of jihad … come and shed blood for the sake of establishing Allah's law."* Moreover, he declared jihad against the Egypt army to be *"a religious duty and divine obligation."*

"Every Muslim must support them according to his ability. Whoever is able to travel to them, fight with them, and increase their ranks, it is a duty to do so … whoever is unable must support them with money, by inciting to fight [with them], and by [helping to] prepare the fighters," Shinqiti stated.

With regard to ongoing Egyptian military operations in the Sinai, al Shinqiti contended that they are merely an attempt to protect Israel. *"The goal of the security campaign that the tyrannical army in Egypt is directing in the Sinai is to protect Israel and its borders after jihadi groups in the Sinai became a real threat to it,"* Shinqiti wrote.

In addition, Shinqiti praised ongoing attacks by "your mujahideen brothers" in the Sinai and called on Egyptian Muslims to join them, *"support them, increase their ranks, and be an aid and a champion of them."* *"[J]ihad in the Sinai is a great opportunity for you to gather and unite under a pure flag, unsullied by ignorant slogans,"* Shinqiti claimed.

Since the overthrow of Mohammed Morsi in early July 2013, there has been a plethora of statements from jihadists in response to the ongoing crackdown on the Muslim Brotherhood. For example, Harith bin Ghazi al Nadhari (also known as Muhammad al Murshidi), an official in al Qaeda in the Arabian Peninsula (AQAP), charged on Aug. 25 that the Egyptian government was seeking *"to return Egypt to the era of oppression, tyranny and the domination of the security and intelligence agencies."*

On Aug. 17, jihadist ideologue Abu Sa'ad al 'Amili posted a series of tweets to his Twitter account urging Egyptian Muslims to prepare for an "open war." Likewise, Abdullah Muhammad Mahmoud of the jihadist Dawa'at al-Haq Foundation for Studies and Research warned Egyptian Muslims, in an article posted to jihadist forums on Aug. 14, that "if you don't do jihad today, then only blame yourselves tomorrow."

Similarly, on Aug. 15, Abu Hafs al Maqdisi, the leader of the Gaza-based Jaish al Ummah (Army of the Nation), called on Egyptians to wage "jihad" against Egyptian army commander General Abdul Fattah el Sisi. Four days later, Shabaab, al Qaeda's affiliate in Somalia, urged Egyptian Muslims to "pick up arms and defend yourself." In addition, on Aug. 30, the Islamic State of Iraq and the Levant called on Egyptians to wage 'jihad' against army.

And on Aug. 22, al Salafiyya al Jihadiyya in Sinai released a statement that called on Muslims to fight the "apostate" Egyptian army. The communiqué was particularly notable as last fall the group said: *"[T]he army and the police are not our targets and that our weapons are directed at the enemies and the enemies of our Ummah the Jews."* More recently, in mid-May, the jihadist group said: *"[T]he target of the Salafist Jihadist current in Sinai is the Zionist enemy and its operations are directed to them, and the Egyptian soldiers are not a target for us."*

More recently, on Sept. 10, Ansar Jerusalem declared that *"it is obligatory to repulse them [the Egyptian army] and fight them until the command of Allah is fulfilled."* Similarly, on Sept. 15, the Salafi jihadist group declared: *"We in*

AnsarJerusalem and all the mujahideen in Sinai in Egypt as a whole stress that the blood of innocent Muslims will not go in vain."

In addition, on Sept. 22, the Ibn Taymiyyah Media Center (ITMC), a jihadist media unit tied to the MujahideenShura Council in the Environs of Jerusalem, called for jihadists to strike the Egyptian army. Now is the time for the *"mujahideen to hit without fail so as to thwart those criminals from among the Egyptian army,"* the group said. And on Oct. 4, al Salafiyya al Jihadiyya in Sinai threatened to kill anyone found aiding Egyptian security forces.

Along with the calls for attacks, another theme that has been emphasized since the overthrow of Mohammed Morsi is the argument that the Muslim Brotherhood had made a mistake in engaging in the democratic process. This theme is a general jihadi talking point that al Qaeda and its affiliates, such as al Shabaab and al Qaeda in the Islamic Maghreb (AQIM), have pushed repeatedly since Morsi's ouster. In July, AQIM official Abu Abdul Ilah Ahmed al Jijeli said Morsi's overthrow should teach Egyptian Muslims *"that the price for applying principles on the ground is a mountain of body parts and seas of blood, because evil must be killed and not shown mercy, and righteousness must be achieved by cutting the head of those who corrupt and not reason with them."*

An essay released in July by Abu Muhammad al Maqdisi, a global jihadi ideologue and former mentor of Abu Musab al Zarqawi made a similar argument. In the essay, dated July 11, 2013, al Maqdisi contended that armed struggle was the only way to achieve the liberation of Muslim lands. Al Maqdisi further claimed that the ouster of Morsi proved *"the soundness of the jihadi project and the choice of the ammunition box over the ballot box."*

And in his most recent message, which was released to jihadist forums on Oct. 11, al Qaeda emir Ayman al Zawahiri concentrated on Egypt. In the audio message, Zawahiri called on Egyptian Muslims to unite and *"rid Egypt of this criminal gang that jumped on power with iron and fire and took advantage of the concession of some factions in their drooling behind the mirage of the delusional reconciliation."*

Egyptian Counter-terrorist Operations

On April 14, 2014 the Court for Urgent Matters officially labeled Ansar Bayt al-Maqdis a terrorist organization. In May 2014, Egypt's general prosecution referred 200 suspected Ansar Bayt al-Maqdis members to criminal court on charges of committing acts of terror. The Egyptian government has accused the Muslim Brotherhood of supporting militant attacks in Egypt but the Brotherhood has denied any such involvement.

Foreign Ministry spokesperson, Badr Abdel-Atty, said that Egypt had been in contact with many countries in an effort to explain the seriousness of the situation and the US State Department has designated Ansar Bayt al-Maqdis a "foreign terrorist organization."

Egypt joined the US-led international coalition, along with nine other Arab states, to combat the IS. So far, Egyptian officials have said that the country's military will not take part in any combat abroad against the IS and will confront the group using other means, including cutting funding sources or pushing an alternative religious discourse. It is unclear how ABM's declaration of allegiance to the Islamic State will affect Egypt's participation in the efforts against the IS.

The Egyptian military has targeted militant hideouts with helicopters and ground troops, killing scores of militants, according to army statements.

On May 23, 2014 the leader of Ansar Bayt al-Maqdis, Shadi al-Menei, was killed along with three senior members in a security operation. Security forces opened fire on the four men as they were in a car in central Sinai, purportedly preparing to carry out an attack on a gas pipeline.

In October 2014, Egyptian military forces arrested WalidAttalah, the leader of the military wing of Ansar Bayt al-Maqdis in North Sinai. Attalah is of Palestinian origin and received Egyptian citizenship during the era of ousted president, Mohamed Morsi. Attalah is suspected of orchestrating an RPG attack in North Sinai, which killed three policemen and injured seven others.

Following the attacks of October 24, 2014, Sinai was placed under a three-month state of emergency. President el-Sisi also ordered the creation of a 500-meter long buffer zone along the Egyptian border with Gaza in an attempt to quash the illegal tunnel trading between Sinai and the Gaza Strip. According to the Defense Ministry, the tunnels are an important method for "armed Takfiri groups to infiltrate Sinai to supply militants with arms, logistical assistance and shelter after staging their heinous attacks on the Egyptian army."

In a controversial move, the Egyptian army gave over 1,100 families who lived within the buffer zone only 48 hours to evacuate their houses. North Sinai's Governor Abdel Fattah Harhour stated that every family will receive EGP300 (US$40) in housing allowance for three months and further compensation will be given for demolished buildings. However, tribal leaders from the region have expressed their dissatisfaction with the sums offered.

ABM issued a statement on its alleged Twitter account condemning the Egyptian army's recent operations to form a buffer zone on the Rafah-Gaza border. Using strong language, as well as Quranic verses to justify its actions, the group said that the government's decision to evacuate hundreds of houses in the planned buffer zone was only helping the "Jews". The statement added that the buffer zone further tightened the ongoing Israeli blockade of the besieged Palestinian enclave. The group also called on local Sinai tribes to join the fight.

On January 31, 2015, Egypt's President Abdel Fattah al-Sisi established a unified command to combat terrorism east of the Suez Canal, following deadly militant attacks in Sinai. Egypt's Supreme Council of the Armed Forces (SCAF) announced the presidential decree establishing the command. Sisi promoted Third Field Army Commander Osama RoshdyAskar to lieutenant general, who will be in charge of the command.

Conclusions

In the wake of the June 2013 coup against the Mohamed Morsi government, Ansar Bayt al-Maqdis expanded its operations and attacks against security personnel. ABM has faced significant losses as a result of the campaign led by the Egyptian armed forces and it needs both financial and logistical support. Ansar Bayt al-Maqdis pledged its allegiance to the Islamic State in a bid to boost recruitment and bolster its fight against the Egyptian army.

The group also swore allegiance to the Islamic State's leader, Abu Bakr al-Baghdadi, and subsequently adopted the name Wilayat Sinai, representing the annexation of the group and its transformation into a province within al-Baghdadi's unrecognized Caliphate.

The announcement is the most significant pledge of support for the Islamic State in the region outside of Iraq and Syria, suggesting that the group's influence over militant groups is overshadowing its once dominant Al-Qaeda rivals.

A key factor for the IS at this stage is how it can use the sympathy of other Islamist groups, and prove that it is not affected by the international coalition's war and that it is still capable of recruiting new members. ABM's infamous reputation in Egypt made them a key target for IS recruitment.

On January 30, 2015, following the deadly attacks in North Sinai, the Egyptian army said that militant attacks will not deter the armed forces from their "holy duty of uprooting terrorism", and the Egyptian armed forces have responded by waging a military campaign throughout North Sinai, targeting terrorist hideouts using Apache helicopters and ground forces.

The main challenge facing President el-Sisi and the Egyptian security forces is to restore security and stability to Egypt. The latest terrorist in North Sinai proves that Egypt will have to fight a long war of attrition against radical Islamic groups in order to achieve this goal.

Baya

ABM made international headlines in November 2014 when the organization pledged allegiance to the Islamic State (IS) in a nine-minute audio speech released on Twitter. By declaring allegiance to IS, it is believed that ABM will receive resources such as weapons, oil, and money, allowing them to perpetrate additional attacks against the Sinai and Gaza Strip.

In their declaration of allegiance to IS in November 2014, ABM condemned the Muslim Brotherhood's attempts at democracy in Egypt by stating, *"shameful peace will do you no good, nor will blasphemous democracy, and you have seen how it has claimed its upholders and their masters."* The formal relationship between the groups is still unclear, but it is believed that IS provides ABM with weapons, money, and supplies.

Since it's inception, ABM has espoused a similar ideology AQ aiming to liberate Muslims from Western oppression based on radical Islam. While also supporting a Sunni interpretation of Shariah law, ABM has never been an official affiliate of AQ. ABM generally maintains a local focus in their goals, perpetrating attacks primarily in the Sinai Peninsula and the Gaza Strip. A main goal of the organization is to drive the Israeli government from Jerusalem. After the removal of Muslim Brotherhood candidate President Mohammed Morsi in 2013, ABM changed the focus of their attacks to Egyptian security and police forces as revenge for the oppression of Muslim militants.

On January 29, 2015 a series of deadly attacks involving car bombs, mortar fire and ambushes targeted several military and police sites in North Sinai. At least 44 people, including military and police personnel and civilians, were killed and 105 others were injured in the attacks.

This was the first major terrorist attack carried out by Ansar Bayt al-Maqdis, the Islamic State group's Egyptian affiliate, in the Sinai Province (Wilayat Sinai). The group claimed responsibility for the attacks via a Twitter account: "We executed extensive, simultaneous attacks in the cities of El-Arish, Sheikh Zuweid and Rafah". The group said it was retaliating against a government crackdown on supporters of former President Mohamed Morsi.

The deadly attacks in North Sinai suggested that Ansar Bayt al-Maqdis may be following the modus operandi of the Islamic State in Iraq and Syria.

Ansar Bayt al-Maqdis (ABM), Egypt's most dangerous Islamic terrorist group, swore allegiance to the Islamic State on November 3, 2014. The group published a nearly 10-minute long recording on its Twitter account, which stated that: "*After entrusting God we decided to swear allegiance to the emir of the faithful Abu Bakr Al-Baghdadi, caliph of the Muslims in Syria and Iraq and in other countries.*".The recording was later suspended from the account along with other jihadist Web sites and forums.

The next day, ABM issued a short tweet denying the media reports that it had pledged allegiance to the Islamic State. In the tweet, ABM asked the media "to check the accuracy of their sources" and warned that all information from the group would only be released via its official social media sites.

Less than a week after denying the above reports, ABM released an audio clip in which it declared its support for the Islamic State, according to media reports. The nine-minute audio clip was posted on a Twitter account claiming to be ABM's official account. "*In accordance with the teachings of the Prophet, we announce our pledge of allegiance to the caliph Ibrahim Ibn Awad ... to listen and obey him...and we call on all Muslims to pledge allegiance to him,*" a man who reportedly identified himself as part of the group's "information department" said in the recording, in which he referred to the Islamic State leader, Abu Bakr al-Baghdadi, by his adopted name.

The speaker reportedly said that al-Baghdadi was "chosen by God" to establish a new caliphate after "Muslims suffered decades of humiliation." A week later, the group used the same Twitter account to deny reports that it had aligned itself with the Islamic State. According to media reports, the speaker also urged Egyptians to rise up against "the tyrant," allegedly referring to President Abdel-Fattah el-Sisi. "*What are you waiting for, after your honor has been aggressed upon and your sons ' blood has been shed at the hands of this tyrant and his soldiers?*", the spokesperson reportedly said.

Shortly after ABM swore allegiance to the Islamic State, a jihadist Web site posted a statement that it attributed to Abu Mosa'ab al-Maqdisi, a prominent Jordanian jihadist scholar who is seen by many as a source of inspiration for the Islamic State, in which he called on Egyptian jihadists to "take the battle" to Cairo and not stay in the Sinai Peninsula. He added that they should target the economy and the tourism industry by attacking major companies and communication organizations, specifically the Suez Canal and Egyptian businessman, NaguibSawiris.

Al-Maqdisi called on ABM to welcome "their immigrant foreign brother fighters" to Egypt while they can still access the country. He concluded with a warning that those who collude with police should be beheaded.

As a jihadist group that has pledged allegiance to the caliphate, ABM should eventually join the war against the international coalition led by the United States to fight the Islamic State in Iraq and Syria.

Ansar Bayt Al-Maqdis had previously sought inspiration and advice, and received financial aid from the Islamic State in return for the former's continued operations against the Egyptian army.

At the end of August 2013, Egyptian police forces in northern Sinai arrested an individual by the name of Adel Hebara, who they accused of belonging to the Sinai Peninsula and participating in the second Rafah massacre, in which 25 Central Security Forces officers were killed.

In the case against Hebera, the court listened to several telephone calls between Hebara and an IS member in Syria, in which the latter promised to transfer $10,000 in return for the implementation of operations in the Sinai Peninsula and for an oath of allegiance to al-Baghdadi. Hebara accepted the conditions. The IS, for its part, sent messages through its Web site to the "brave mujahedeen of Sinai" in which it called on Sinai militants to keep fighting the Egyptian army and establish an Islamic state in the peninsula. The IS also criticized Al-Qaeda for not fighting against the Egyptian army.

The message stated: *"Keep your faith in the religion of God, may he be praised, and know that you are in the right. Do not slacken, no matter how much people betray you or work against you. Our hearts, men and available resources are at your service, for we all fight to establish the rule of God's laws. God willing, we shall be one to cooperate in enforcing religion, and God will not divide us, neither through borders, nor nationalities, for we are with you in heart, substance, effort and money."*

In September 2014, residents of border villages in Sinai near the cities of Sheikh Zuweid and Rafah reported seeing gunmen wave the black IS flag and carry banners emblazoned with "Islamic State," though the words Iraq and Levant were absent.

Links with Hamas

Analysts have debated the nature of ABM's relationship with several groups, including the Muslim Brotherhood, AQ, and IS. Some claim that ABM is the militant wing of the Muslim Brotherhood. Other analysts dispute this claim, saying that ABM instead is a militant alterative to the Muslim Brotherhood, seeking to draw disenfranchised Brotherhood members away from the group.

In addition, there is speculation about the relationship between ABM and AQ. While the two groups share a similar ideology, they were never formal affiliates. Until Ayman Zawahiri, AQ's leader, mentioned "our people in the Sinai" in January 2014, there had not even been confirmation that AQ recognized ABM. ABM's declaration of allegiance to IS could indicate a split between AQ and ABM. Some ABM cells in the Nile Valley remain loyal to AQ, which could possibly divide the group into two factions: one that remains loyal to AQ and one that is newly loyal to IS.

In September 2013, Egyptian Major General Ahmad Abd al-Halim stated that ABM is part of a larger organization working in the same sphere as Hamas. In addition, ABM's alleged use of smuggling tunnels along the eastern Egypt-Israel border is cited as a link with Hamas.

The question of whether Hamas' military wing cooperated with Wilayat Sinai (literally Sinai Province) is critical for Hamas. This issue is expected to impact not only the future of its relationship with Egypt, but the future of the movement overall. The largest terrorist attack in Sinai occurred when the leaders of the political wing thought the complicated relationship with the regime of Egyptian President Abdel Fattah al-Sisi was stabilizing and that improved relations and a calming of the tensions between them was on the horizon. Once again, however, an accusing finger is pointed toward Hamas, and its leaders are forced to defend themselves.

The leaders of the movement, Ismail Haniyeh, Mousa Abu Marzouk and Abu Obeida, the spokesman of the military wing, quickly denied any connection with the Sinai terror organization affiliated with the Islamic State (IS). In an interview with Al-Quds network, Abu Marzouk explained that everyone knows how his movement works in Gaza against what he called "the black extremism." He was referring to the surge of arrests in recent weeks carried out by Hamas of members of Salafist organizations in Gaza after Salafists had fired rockets toward Israel and tried to entangle his movement. Israel repeatedly states that it holds Hamas responsible for rockets fired at it.

Abu Marzouk, considered to have good relations with the Sisi regime, was sent on a defensive propaganda mission, while Khaled Meshaal, the leader of the movement, who is treated as persona non grata by Egypt, kept his silence. Any word from him would probably cause further damage to the complex relations.

Abu Marzouk, who has filled the leadership void in the movement ever since the crisis with Egypt, did his utmost to diminish the tension between the sides. He claimed that not only did Hamas have no interest in cooperating with the terrorists in Sinai, but the movement itself was harmed by the terror attack on its border. Abu Marzouk argued that every time the Egyptians intend to open the Rafah crossing a horrible attack happens and disrupts things. "This is detrimental to the security of Palestinians, especially those living in Gaza," he added, saying that the attacks hurt Hamas' relations with Egypt.

On the other hand, the coordinator of government activities in the territories, Maj. Gen. Yoav (Poli) Mordechai, was interviewed on Al Jazeera in Arabic and asserted that Israel has intelligence information that Hamas supports the Wilayat Sinai group, which carried out the attack, and even helped it with weapons. Mordechai added that WaelFaraj, a commander of a unit of Hamas' military wing, Izz ad-Din al-Qassam Brigades, smuggled injured fighters of the jihadi group to hospitals in Gaza and that the members of the military wing have close ties with the organization, which is affiliated with IS.

The Egyptian response to Hamas' alleged involvement was restrained. Sisi, who arrived for a tour of Sinai, did not rush to accuse members of al-Qassam Brigades of cooperation with the perpetrators of the attack, but the leaders of the movement also know that the crisis hasn't passed. The Egyptians haven't yet cleared the movement of responsibility, and Hamas believes Israel will try to convince Egypt that it has evidence of such cooperation. Hamas believes Israel wants to drive a wedge between Hamas and Cairo to destroy the bridge they have started to build into the heart of the Egyptian regime in the last few months.

In any case, the leaders of Hamas will find it hard to dispel all blame from themselves. In recent weeks, a number of people who were hurt in altercations with Egyptian security forces in Sinai have been brought to the al-Najjar hospital in Rafah in the Gaza Strip. The information about al-Qassam Brigades bringing these wounded persons to the hospital wasn't kept secret. Residents of Rafah saw how wounded people were brought in Hamas "military" vehicles and treated by a select medical staff.

A senior security figure in the Palestinian Authority, who is following events in Gaza, told that the cooperation of members of al-Qassam Brigades with many armed groups in the Sinai Peninsula is well-known to the leadership of the Palestinian Authority, Israeli intelligence, as well as Egyptian intelligence. He says the information shared by everyone isn't a working assumption, but well-founded and well-known, and that it includes the names of people active on both sides.

The activity of Faraj, which Mordechai revealed on Al Jazeera, is known and has taken place for a long time. According to the source, for years the leaders of the military wing carried out extensive smuggling operations with anyone who could help Hamas in Sinai before Israel's disengagement from Gaza (2005), but especially after the tightening of the siege on the Gaza Strip.

The close relations reached a peak after the fall of the Muslim Brotherhood regime in Egypt in July 2013, with the ascension of Sisi, a general who then headed the Egyptian military. After the Egyptian military sealed the smuggling tunnels with Egypt in Rafah and created a buffer zone, a strategic change occurred in the way in which Hamas' military wing perceived the Egyptian security forces. The Egyptian military is now perceived by the armed groups in Sinai and the Gaza Strip, including Hamas, as an enemy, and their goal has become to strike it and weaken its power in Sinai.

For years, a complicated and mutually beneficial relationship was built between Hamas members and jihadi activists on the Sinai Peninsula. Al-Qassam Brigades received aid from IS affiliates such as Wilayat Sinai, Aknaf Bayt al-Maqdis battalion and other terror organizations in smuggling arms, ammunition and raw materials such as fuel and building materials into Gaza. In exchange, Hamas provided a significant percentage of the arms smuggled from Sudan and Libya. Thus a reciprocal relationship was created that no one among the political leadership of Hamas will be able to uproot.

This utilitarian relationship structure is known and familiar to the heads of the political leadership of Hamas. Ever since Israel placed a siege on Gaza in June 2007, they encouraged the heads of al-Qassam Brigades to conduct the Saladin project — the creation of the smuggling tunnel network between Egypt and

Israel. Any means were acceptable for that purpose, including the deliberate connection to "black extremism."

Russian boots in Syria

The positioning of Russian aircraft in Syria gives the Kremlin an ability to shape and control U.S. and Western operations in both Syria and Iraq out of all proportion to the size of the Russian force. It can compel the U.S. to accept a de facto combined coalition with Russia, Syria, Iran, and Lebanese Hezbollah, possibly in support of indiscriminate operations against any and all regime opponents, not just ISIS and Jabhat al-Nusra. It may portend the establishment of a permanent Russian air and naval base in the Eastern Mediterranean. Russian forces have prepared and trained to conduct close air support and possibly special operations in Syria, and may begin doing so within days.

The deployment of Russian military forces to Syria is a major geostrategic inflection. Its significance goes far beyond the situation in Syria. It may well herald, in fact, a new era in global geopolitics and security. Russian forces are establishing an airbase likely to become capable of conducting operations throughout the Levant and the Eastern Mediterranean. It would be the first time in history that Russia had an outpost on land for projecting force beyond the confines of the Black Sea. The U.S. and NATO must consider and respond to this development recognizing its true stakes.

The Obama Administration remains inexplicably bewildered, however. Secretary of State John Kerry stated on 22 September 2015 that the Russian equipment that had arrived in Syria was there to protect Russian forces. "We don't yet have clarity with respect to the Russian effort," he noted in a press conference. After Kerry's meeting with Russian Foreign Minister Sergei Lavrov on 27 September 2015, the State Department stated: "Again, we're just at the beginning of trying to understand what the Russians' intentions are in Syria, in Iraq, and to try to see if there are mutually beneficial ways forward here."

Understanding the Kremlin's intentions at a basic level is not really very hard, though. Russian President Vladimir Putin certainly means to deter the U.S.-led coalition from attacking the forces of Syrian President Bashar al Assad, establishing any sort of no-fly zone, or taking any meaningful action that might harm Assad's forces. He also means to forge a counter-alliance consisting of Russia, Iran, Iraq, Syria, and Lebanese Hezbollah and demonstrate that his coalition is more effective than the West's. He intends, finally, to establish a permanent foothold in the Middle East from which he can threaten NATO's southern flank directly, project power into the Mediterranean and the Arab

World, and generally re-create Russia's aura as a global power. He may have more complicated objectives in mind as well, but the State Department should be able at least to recognize these.

Americans should not fall for Putin's "active measures," a phrase he used in his interview with Charlie Rose on 60 Minutes to dismiss as falsehoods descriptions of the Assad regime's brutality against the Syrian people. One must reckon with such an aptitude for falsehood when hearing Putin state, "we do not have any obsession with being a superpower in the international arena." And one must hear the threat in statements such as, "Russia will not participate in any troop operations in the territory of Syria or in any other states. Well, at least we don't plan on it right now....

The Russian deployment severely constrains Western options within Syria and may come to challenge America's ability to continue to operate in Iraq as well. Russian aircraft flying around Syria give Moscow absolute veto power over any attempt to establish any sort of no-fly zone or ISIS-free zone, unless the U.S. and its partners are prepared to risk aerial combat with the Russian Air Force. Russian planes can escort Syrian Air Force (SAF) aircraft on missions, fly combat air patrols (CAP) to protect Syrian helicopters engaged in barrel-bombing, and harass U.S. or NATO aircraft or drones attempting to enforce ISIS-free zones.

Putin is likely trying to guarantee that the U.S. cannot attack the Assad regime effectively now or in the future. The Russian presence alone helps to deter any strikes against Assad. If the U.S. begins to coordinate its air operations with the Russians and the Russians remain tightly allied with Assad, it stands to reason that Moscow will pass along to Damascus warning of any potential U.S. attack. Considering the increasing closeness of the Russia-Iran relationship, we can assume that Putin would provide a similar benefit to Iranian and Lebanese Hezbollah forces on the ground in Syria. The Iraqi military has already announced that it will share intelligence with Syria, Russia, and Iran.

The composition of Russian forces deployed to Syria is absurdly large to be simply protecting Russian civilian and military positions already there. It is, rather, consistent with the mission of providing air support to Assad regime ground forces fighting against the rebels. Su-25 (Frogfoot) ground-attack aircraft comprise the majority of the fixed-wing airframes visible on the ground at Bassel al Assad airfield near Latakia on the Syrian coast.

These planes are similar to U.S. Air Force A-10s in that they were designed to fly low and slow to provide close-air support (CAS) to ground forces engaged with enemy units. The Mi-24 Hind helicopter is a large attack platform that performs a role similar to that of the U.S. Apache, except that the Hind is much larger and, unlike the Apache, can carry troops and supplies as well as conduct ground-attack missions.

These are among the premier Russian airframes for supporting troops in contact. They have limited combat radii (400 kilometers or less) and so would not be ideal for operations beyond the line from roughly Qusayr in the south to Idlib in the north from their current position. They could be moved to other Syrian regime airbases, particularly Damascus and Der ezZour to support operations in southern or eastern Syria. They pose a very limited threat to U.S., forces, Turkey, Jordan, or Israel from Latakia.

Moscow has also positioned a smaller number of Su-24 Fencer and Su-30 Flanker multirole fighters at Latakia, however. The Fencer is an old airframe used mainly for longer-range ground-attack missions. Its combat radius is sufficient to cover much of Syria from the base at Latakia and to range into the Eastern Mediterranean as well.

It can conduct long-range strike missions against specific targets or aerial reconnaissance. It is not a serious threat to the ability of U.S., NATO, or Israeli air forces to operate freely throughout the region, however, nor is it particularly survivable against advanced surface-to-air missiles. The Flanker is another story entirely. Its radius of action is several thousand kilometers, and it is very well-designed for aerial maneuvering, making it much more able to avoid SAMs and theoretically more capable of contesting airspace against limited numbers of less-proficient Western aircraft. It can be used for strike operations anywhere throughout the Levant and can also perform reconnaissance missions over a wide area.

The Fencers and Flankers are a sensible part of an air posture aimed exclusively at supporting the Assad regime, despite their advanced capabilities and long ranges that might appear to transcend local requirements. Long ranges also translate into the ability to stay airborne for a long time waiting for targets to appear—or to conduct reconnaissance over a given area. The more advanced technical capabilities, particularly of the Flankers, could well allow the Russians to provide much more timely and accurate support to ground forces than the Frogfoots could do, particularly at short notice far from their base. The air package visible on the ground so far, therefore, remains entirely consistent with an exclusively local mission.

U.S. forces undertaking a similar mission would likely bring to bear a mix of aircraft with similar capabilities, ranging from A-10s to advanced and long-range F-15s and F/A-18s.

The U.S. would similarly undertake to expand the ground support facilities at an airbase it intended to use for a protracted support mission, as the Russians are doing. Satellite imagery shows fuel and weapons storage facilities, radomes, logistics areas, and a relatively small complement of (probably) T-90 tanks, advanced BTR-80 armored personnel carriers, and artillery—all consistent with the requirements to keep combat aircraft flying and to secure the airfield against possible terrorist or even insurgent attacks.

Such U.S. activities nevertheless distress regional competitors even when they are aimed entirely at narrowly-constrained local operations. The Iranian military felt itself surrounded when American aircraft were operating out of bases in both Afghanistan and Iran, and even built out additional airfields of its own along the Afghan border to defend against the possibility that U.S. planes would one day fly west rather than east

The U.S. and its NATO and non-NATO partners should take a similar view of the development of the Bassel al Assad airfield into a major Russian airbase. Moscow may well intend at this point nothing more than helping keep Assad in power, but the airßeld, particularly if advanced, long-range, multi-role fighters like the Flanker stay there, gives Vladimir Putin dramatic new capabilities against Turkey, Israel, and the U.S. Sixth Fleet.

The location and orientation of the airfield is particularly problematic in this regard, should Putin choose to use it as a way of increasing tensions with the West outside of Ukraine. The airbase is less than 50 kilometers from the Turkish border and the runways point north-south. A supersonic fighter, such as the Flanker, taking off to the north could be in Turkish airspace within minutes. Worse still, it could be almost impossible to tell if such a fighter intended to cross into Turkey or turn east to operate against rebels until the very last moment. Turkish Air Force aircraft and the U.S. and European NATO planes deployed in Turkey would have very little time to decide whether to intercept the Russian planes or allow them to fly into Turkey.

Such considerations are far from theoretical, considering the aggressiveness with which Russian military aircraft have been regularly oveflying the Baltic countries, Sweden, and Finland. The Bassel al-Assad airbase allows Putin to extend this pattern to Turkey, Israel, Jordan, and Saudi Arabia if he chose.

It also would allow his aircraft to shadow the U.S. Sixth Fleet around the Eastern Mediterranean. He could force Turkey and its NATO allies to establish standing combat air patrols along the southern Turkish border. If he kept the tension very high, the risk of mistakes and accidental weapons releases would also increase. The Russian invasion of Crimea and crypto-invasion of Ukraine has forced the U.S. and Europeans to think about potential territorial violations in northern or eastern Europe that might invoke the Article V collective defense provisions requiring all allies to come to the defense of a threatened member.

They have prepared for such contingencies through the pre-deployment of units and armor in order to deter or respond. Turkey is also a NATO ally, and Russia's presence on the Turkish border gives Putin the ability to test whether NATO will indeed invoke and support Article V in a very different context for which the alliance is much less prepared.

The presence of the Flankers in Latakia could also allow Putin to expand his interference into Iraq. Flankers or even Fencers could pursue ISIS fighters across the border, which they cross freely, to short distances at first, but ultimately deeper into Anbar, Ninewah, and Salah-ad-Din Provinces as well— even over Baghdad International Airport. He might work with his Iranian allies to cause the Iraqi government to invite or, at least, consent to Russian air operations against ISIS in Iraq. Iraq, after all, has no ability of its own to contest such operations even though it retains full legal authority over its own airspace.

If U.S. aircraft wanted to intercept Russian planes flying into Iraq, they would require the permission of the Iraqi government to do so. It is highly unlikely that any Iraqi government would put itself so clearly on the side of the U.S. and against the Russians and Iranians under the current circumstances. The U.S. might well end itself obliged to contend with competing Russian air operations over both Iraq and Syria.

That will not be easy to do. Coordinating the activities of many high-performance aircraft in a confined space is an intricate and difficult job under the best of circumstances. Differences in approach between the U.S. Marine Corps and the U.S. Air Force and Navy, in fact, were sufficient to make it desirable to designate Marine-only airspace in Iraq and Afghanistan. How will American and Russian aircraft conflict their operations? The easiest and most tempting way will be to designate, at least informally, areas in which

Russian aircraft but not Western aircraft fly, and vice-versa. But Putin can force continued renegotiation of such delineations at any time simply by ordering his planes to fly beyond their allotted zone. If he causes them to operate broadly across Syria or into Iraq he can attempt to compel the U.S. to establish de facto a more integrated approach to air operations—one that might effectively require U.S. aircraft to tell the Russians of planned operations in advance.

Putin may be positioning himself, therefore, to compel the U.S. to merge its coalition with his simply in order to mitigate the risks caused by having a lot of combat aircraft flying around. Putin can thus try to take effective control of U.S. air operations in Iraq and Syria without ever having to issue an order. Such an idea is not theoretical either.

It would be an implementation of the doctrine of "reflexive control" that is well and prominently established in current Russian military thinking and is in active use in Russian operations against Ukraine. The idea behind reflexive control is to shape the environment in such a way that the enemy chooses Russia's preferred course of action voluntarily, because it is easiest and all the others appear much more difficult and risky, if not impossible. Reflexive control allows a much weaker force to constrain and even control the activities of a much stronger force. It has worked magnificently in Ukraine, and Putin may well be trying to expand it to the Levant and Iraq.

The U.S. already seems to be falling into this trap. A senior State Department official offering a read-out of the September 27 discussion between Secretary Kerry and Foreign Minister Lavrov said, "if the Russians are going to be more engaged in this theater, we have to de-conflict militarily."

De-confliction is a form of military cooperation that gives the less-responsible party leverage over the more-responsible party. Western air forces are not likely to be willing to take risks that Russian aircraft might. Thus Moscow will control what "de-confliction" actually means in the skies over Syria...or Iraq. This is part of reflexive control at work.

The Russian military has just completed a major annual exercise, Center-2015, which it claims involved 95,000 troops. The kinds of training it reportedly executed offer some useful clues about the types of activities its forces might be prepared to undertake in Syria, although the fact that it claims its forces conducted certain types of training does not mean they did, and the fact that they trained does not mean that they could execute in combat. The breadth and specificity of the claims are nevertheless interesting in what they reveal about possible Russian intentions or, at least, capabilities, for operations in Syria.

Russia exercised its Hind attack helicopters extensively, for example. They practiced conducting rocket and bombing runs against ground targets and providing air cover to ground forces flying very-low-altitude nap-of-the-earth missions. They fired their unguided rockets and cannons against targets mimicking columns of military equipment. They practiced flying with one engine off (simulating its failure in flight) at 200 meters.

These are the kinds of skills that would be required if the Russians intended to provide close air support to Syrian, Iranian, or Lebanese Hezbollahi troops in contact with rebel forces.

Russian special forces units, known as Spetsnaz, have also been honing their skills. A group from the Russian military base in Abkhazia (which Russia seized from Georgia in the 2008 war) practiced ambushing and seizing a source, attacking another facility based on his information, and then returning to base to conduct document exploitation of the captured material. A combined force of Spetsnaz and military police practiced fighting "illegal armed formations" in an urban setting. The exercise included freeing ten hostages and destroying the bad guys, while the military police worked to re-establish order and control road movements. Russian reconnaissance units are also practicing operations in mountainous terrain both in North Ossetia (in the Caucasus) and in Tajikistan (where a Russian military force is permanently based).

Russian airborne forces practiced air-dropping into enemy areas to conduct reconnaissance and the destruction of illegal armed groups. They exercised in different drop zones each time, from low altitudes, and into areas unknown to the troops.

All of these advanced skills would be valuable should the Russians deploy Spetsnaz or other elite formations into Syria to conduct missions similar to those executed by U.S. Special Forces against high-value targets.

The Russians have also been practicing air operations of many varieties. Their fighters have exercised escort missions for long-range bombers (which would also be applicable to escorting any other kind of aircraft facing potential air threats, such as Assad's air force should the West declare a no-fly zone).

The Russian Ministry of Defense reported on September 21/2015 seemingly apropos of nothing, that forces of the Southern Military District had conducted more than 20 exercises "of various scales" with the "newest ground-attack aircraft Su-25SM", which the Russians call "Grach" or "Rook," and NATO calls Frogfoot.

These exercises included attacking enemy aircraft on the ground, "bases of illegal armed formations," and weapons depots. Frogfoot crews in particular practiced destroying concealed insurgent bases in forested and mountainous regions, as well as emergency actions in the case of equipment failure, and concealed movement to avoid the attacks of hostile fighters. They conducted these training exercises at low altitude and with an eye to defending themselves against anti-aircraft weapons that the enemy might have.

The crews of Su-24 Fencer aircraft practiced aerial refueling, a skill that could be very important indeed if the Russians intend to keep those aircraft flying over Syria for extended periods of time.

All of these exercises support operations in which Russian forces are already engaged in Ukraine, of course. They are also good preparation for counter-terrorism operations against the ISIS affiliate in the Caucasus. It is easy to argue that Putin is only preparing to help the U.S. accomplish something we have been too timid to do—defeat ISIS. Russian aircraft and helicopters will presumably not face the same extreme restrictions on dropping weapons when they might cause civilian casualties or when they are not certain of the target that hamper American crews. And Russia's alliance with Assad virtually ensures much more effective coordination of ground and air operations against whatever rebels the Syrian regime chooses to fight. Might Russia's intervention not work out for the U.S. after all?

The answer is absolutely not. Putin is not simply intervening to attack ISIS. His stated goal and posture is to support the Assad regime and Bashar al Assad in particular. The deployment of Russian forces into Syria therefore effectively guarantees that Assad can remain in power for as long as Putin chooses to back him, thus obviating the need for Assad to make any meaningful concessions to the opposition. Assad's forces had been reeling from the advances of multiple rebel groups and running out of reinforcements. His regime might have faced collapse, he might have been pushed aside, or he might have felt compelled to negotiate seriously with his Syrian opponents.

Now he is likely to become extremely intransigent. The only path to ending the war thus offered by this Russian adventure is the crushing of the majority Sunni Arab population in Syria by the combined forces of Assad, Iran, Lebanese Hezbollah, and the Kremlin. It is hard to see that approach being successful. The Russians, after all, tried something like it in Afghanistan in the 1980s. The conditions in Syria today are not more propitious than they were then—and Russia is nothing like as strong militarily as was the Soviet Union at the height of its power. No, the advent of Russian reinforcements is likely only to cement a brutal stalemate that has driven millions of people from their homes, radicalized the region, caused a humanitarian apocalypse, and turned Syria into a magnet for global jihadists.

Any serious plan for bringing peace, ultimately, to Syria requires separating supporters of ISIS and al Qaeda affiliate Jabhat alNusra from the bulk of the Syrian Sunni Arab population now working with them for lack of any better alternatives. That approach requires differentiating among the various groups fighting against Assad, identifying which ones might be lured away, and determining what would be required to lure them. Putin, it seems clear, has no interest whatsoever in such an approach. He told U.S. networks that "provision of military support to illegal structures runs counter to the principles of modern international law and the United Nations Charter," and made it clear that he regards the only "legitimate government entities" in Syria to be the organs of Assad's government.

It is likely, therefore, that Russian support for Assad will take the form of an indiscriminate attack against Assad's opponents, regardless of the degree of their affiliation with ISIS or JN. Such an effort will tend to unify the Syrian opposition with the jihadists against the Russians and Assad. If the U.S. appears to support Russia—a position the Obama Administration seems to be steadily drifting toward—it will solidify the idea that all of the Western powers are united with Iran behind Assad and that only al Qaeda and ISIS offer international support for the struggle against the Alawite government. A blank-check support for the Assad regime of the sort Putin is ready to provide, in other words, is very likely to backfire, further radicalizing the conflict and permitting the continued commitment of war crimes by the Assad regime.

The Russian deployment to Syria is a serious blow to the U.S., its allies, and its prospects for developing and executing any plausible strategy to defeat ISIS and al Qaeda in the Levant and Iraq. It is likely the thin edge of the wedge, moreover, that will offer Putin greater opportunities to disrupt American operations in the Middle East and the Mediterranean. The path of least resistance for the U.S. will be gradually coming to terms with the new reality and making a virtue of necessity by cooperating, reluctantly at first and then more enthusiastically, with the Russian-Iranian-Syrian axis that is now forming.

It will, in other words, continue the trend of realigning the American geostrategic position the Middle East fundamentally. More remarkably, it may represent the opening of a new Russian flank against NATO and against America's ability to operate in the region. If so, it will be much easier to resist or defect this Russian adventure now, at its beginning and when it is very limited, than to reverse it some years hence after it has taken form root.

The battle begins

Before dawn on Thursday, Sept. 24/2015, Russian marines went into battle for the first time since their deployment to Syria. Russian Marine Brigade 810 fought with Syrian army and Hizballahspecial forces in an attack on ISIS forces at the Kweiris airbase, east of Aleppo.

This operation runs contrary to the assurances of President Vladimir Putin to Prime Minister Binyamin Netanyahu on Sept. 21/2015 – just three days ago - that Russian forces in Syria were only there to defend Russian interests and would not engaged in combat with the Syrian army, Hizballah or Iranian troops. The ISIS force defending the air base is dominated by Chechen fighters under the command of Abu Omar al-Shishani, who is considered one of the terrorist organization's leading commanders in the last two years. The 27-year-old al-Shishani hails from the Chechen enclave of Pankisi in Georgia, like many others who joined ISIS from 2012.

However, targeting Chechen fighters was not the only reason for the order given by Russian command in Syria to attack the air base. The Russian mission in Syria would be to break the Syrian rebel siege on Aleppo, Syria's second-largest city. As their first step, the Russians would have to prevent the cutoff of highway 5, running from Aleppo to Damascus, and keep it open for Syrian army reinforcements and military equipment to the city.

The build-up at Latakia

It's been evident since late August that Israel expected the imminent deployment of Russian fighter squadrons - the Americans chose to stall for a few days before giving any response to these early stories, mindful presumably that President Putin was about to commit on the ground in a way President Obama has dreaded doing since the outbreak of the Syrian civil war four years ago. From 20 August shipments of equipment from Black Sea ports, via the Bosphorus, to the Syrian port of Tartous started picking up.

The operation followed a logical military pattern: secure the Latakia airfield; improve its facilities; create a defence against possible air attack; and lastly, bring in your combat aircraft. Then dozens of flights by heavy Antonov cargo planes started augmenting the sea lift.

The Russians had moved in 28 combat jets (12 Su24 bombers, 12 Su25 ground attack aircraft and 4 Su-30 multi-role fighters), two types of drones, and 20 helicopters (a mix of gunships and troop carriers). Some reports suggest that the deployment is getting so large that it will need more than one airfield for its operations, and indeed the latest satellite pictures of the Syrian coastal region suggest that other military facilities may be under preparation for further deployments.

Pentagon officials were briefing on Monday, that the drones were already operating, presumably searching for targets, and that offensive air operations could be expected "within days". The Russians, in a fortnight, have moved in a striking force of roughly equivalent power to the few dozen surviving capable aircraft at Syria's disposal - but with more modern guided weapons and surveillance systems. This initiative, just like the Kremlin's moves in Ukraine last year, strikes at a delicate transatlantic seam.

The deployment of some of Russia's most advanced ground attack planes and fighter jets as well as multiple air defense systems at the base near the ancestral home of President Bashar al-Assad appears to leave little doubt about Moscow's goal to establish a military outpost in the Middle East. The planes are protected by at least two or possibly three SA-22 surface-to-air, antiaircraft systems, and unarmed Predator-like surveillance drones are being used to fly reconnaissance missions.

With competent pilots and with an effective command and control process, the addition of these aircraft could prove very effective depending on the desired objectives for their use. In addition, a total of 15 Russian Hip transport and

Hind attack helicopters are also now stationed at the base, doubling the number of those aircraft from last week. For use in possible ground attacks, the Russians now also have nine T-90 tanks and more than 500 marines, up from more than 200 last week.

The operation to move dozens of combat aircraft and hundreds of troops to the aid of President Bashar al-Assad must have been given the green light some weeks ago, but think of what's been happening during the past 10 days as reports emerged of the Russians appearing at an air base near the Assad stronghold of Latakia.

White House's "no way" policy

A major overhaul of the Obama administration's program to train and equip moderate Syrian rebels is expected to be announced in the coming days, according to several administration officials.

The move comes after the program has fallen far short of its goals. A top U.S. general told the Senate on Wednesday that of the thousands the Pentagon was supposed to train in the first year, only four or five are in place on the battlefield.

One leading option to dramatically reshape the train-and-equip program would be to place several hundred trained rebels with other groups of Syrian fighters to fight ISIS.

The trained rebels might not fight ISIS directly, as the program originally intended, but instead would help by providing communications, intelligence and targeting information, officials said, though they would not call in airstrikes on their own. Standard procedure continues to be that coalition forces verify all information before airstrikes are conducted.

The administration is looking at potentially placing the trained rebels with groups of Syrian Arabs now living in the areas between Raqqa and the Turkish border, as well as alongside some Kurds in the area. Officials said that there may be a loose coalition of hundreds of Syrian Arabs willing to join forces.

No final decision has been made, and other options remain under consideration. But the overhaul underscores the conclusion inside the administration that the program as it currently exists "is a big mess" and must be changed, one official told CNN.

A review of the effort has been underway since the initial group of some 54 rebels put into northern Syria this summer came under attack and are no longer a functioning fighting force. That attack demonstrated that units have to be larger so the forces can protect themselves, officials said.

The fate of the original effort to train and equip more than 5,000 moderate rebels in the first year was the subject of a fiery hearing before the Senate Armed Services Committee when the top U.S. general in charge of fighting ISIS acknowledged the current status of the initial 54 trained by the United States.

With American policy stalled and arguments about the degree to which its bombing campaign has blunted Islamic State (IS), the president's envoy, retired General John Allen, and several other senior officials have decided to step down. Gen Allen was known to believe the US should harden its position on the overthrow of President Assad, and in the need for a safe zone in the north of Syria - instead the prospect seems to be slipping away of either happening.

The US general running Central Command, the Pentagon's Middle East arm, went through humiliating testimony in front of the Senate Armed Services Committee in which he had to admit that the number of Syrian rebels trained under a $500m (£325m) US program who had actually made it into the field could be counted on the fingers of one hand, and that plans for a safe area in northern Syria to protect civilians would be meaningless without ground troops, but he could not recommend the commitment of US soldiers on such a mission.

IS has been spreading its influence among Muslim communities in Russia's North Caucasus, and many of the Russians in its ranks are believed to be Chechens. An anti-Moscow insurgency continues in the region.

The main nationalities of IS volunteers from Central Asia are Uzbek, Kazakh and Turkmen.

Russia's "Syria stake"

US Secretary of Defence Ashton Carter and Russia's Defence Minister Sergei Shoigu have held their first talks to discuss the conflict in Syria.The phone call between the two men which took place on Friday, with Russian state media saying it proved the two sides had common ground, while the Pentagon said the ministers discussed how the US and Russia could avoid accidentally clashing on the ground.

Russia's reported increased military presence in Syria has raised concerns in the US for some time. First and foremost are what the leadership perceives as security concerns. The Kremlin argues that the fall of Syrian President Bashar al-Assad would bring radical Islamists to power in Syria and that this in turn would lead to further destabilisation in the Middle East and consequently affect Russia's Muslim regions.

Russia points to Western-backed changes of government in Iraq and Libya, which have led to violence and instability affecting the region as a whole. Moscow is also concerned about the possible return to Russia of the 2,000 or more Russian-speakers currently fighting against Assad's forces.

Russia's economic and military interests also play a role. Ambitions to extend the reach of the Russian navy mean Moscow needs to safeguard the supply point in Tartus, while Russian energy companies are interested in the possible oil and gas reserves along Syria's coastline.

For these reasons, Moscow's "master plan" is to ensure the survival of the Assad regime, and recent reports of its decision to increase military support to Damascus should therefore not have come as a surprise to the West. The Kremlin is not unwavering in its loyalty to President Assad. On the contrary, his inflexibility irritates the Kremlin and has created mistrust on several occasions prior to the current conflict, including in the early 2000s, when the Syrian government refused to extradite Chechen rebels.

Russian contacts with the Syrian opposition demonstrate that Moscow is keeping its options open. But the Russian government would probably show more flexibility if the opposition offered to preserve some of Russia's political and economic influence in a post-Assad Syria, and to prevent an influx of jihadist groups from Syria to Russia's Muslim regions.

In June 2015, while confirming Moscow's support for Damascus, President Putin stated that the Kremlin was "ready to work with the president [Assad] to ensure political transformation, so that all Syrians have access to the instruments of power".

In this vein, the Kremlin has adopted a two-track approach. On the one hand it is intensifying dialogue with the international community on options for the national reconciliation process in Syria. Meanwhile, it is increasing the volume and quality of military supplies to the Syrian regime to ensure it survives long enough for the Kremlin to achieve a diplomatic breakthrough commensurate with its interests.

Russia's reaction

Russia's reaction would be likely to be overwhelmingly negative. In 2013, when the US and its partners were considering options for military intervention, Foreign Minister Sergei Lavrov and Defence Minister Shoigu said Moscow would adopt an asymmetric response to any attack on Assad, to make the West "learn its lesson".

The increased supplies of arms and weapons systems provided by Moscow will make any military operation against Damascus more challenging. Despite the presence of Russian military advisers and other troops, any direct military confrontation between Russia and Western forces in Syria is unlikely though.

This telephone call, initiated by the Russian side, shows that Moscow does not want to escalate confrontation with the West over Syria beyond the current level without what it sees as good reason.

Currently, the Russian authorities are doing their best to clarify their position and partly allay Western concerns. As part of possible trust-building measures they even offered to launch direct negotiations with the US on how to deal with the so-called Islamic State (IS).
Russia's endgame

The confrontation between Russia and the West over Ukraine has contributed to Moscow's heightened engagement in the Middle East. The Kremlin believes that good relations with states in the region can help Russia avoid international isolation and compensate for the negative effect of US and EU sanctions.

If necessary, the Kremlin can also use its leverage with other states in the region, such as Iran and Egypt, to put additional pressure on Western countries.

For example, in March 2014, in the wake of the Ukrainian crisis, Russia announced it was reconsidering its participation in the negotiations between Iran and the P5+1 (the five permanent members of the UN Security Council - China, France, Russia, the UK and the US - plus Germany). This was enough to keep Washington concerned about this possibility for the rest of 2014.

"We don't want to die there"

Mainly non commissioned troops refused to deploy to Syria due to their fear of ISIS. One of the soldiers, a lieutenant named Alexei, said, "We don't want to go Syria, we don't want to die there."

The group complained that the military had hid their destination from them. They were due to be shipped off on September 17, but 10 days later they were told they would be deployed to a hot region with a very different climate than what they were used to, and that there would be poisonous animals at the new place, but the specific region was not named.

At first, the soldiers assumed they were being sent to eastern Ukraine. But On September 16, the army told them they would be sent to Latakia and that they may have to participate in the fighting alongside Syrian troops.

The troops were required to sign confidentiality agreements, and were told that if they didn't sign – their families would not receive compensation if they were wounded or killed in the fighting. The soldiers were also warned that if they didn't sign – they would face criminal charges.

The soldiers were surprised to receive new weapons and equipment with their serial numbers removed. The soldiers were also instructed on how to behave if they were captured.

Mothers of soldiers had been sent to Syria, said that their sons had been sent to fight a war that was not theirs: "People there are driven like cattle to the slaughter." The soldiers complained that they felt like mercenaries.

Alex Tanzer, an expert on Russian media, explained that President Vladimir Putin passed a law in recent months which banned the publication of names of soldiers killed in action. The law was passed as a result of the public outcry caused by the war in Ukraine. The outcry has been renewed by the soldiers who are being sent to Syria. The Russian Defense Ministry declined to comment on the report.

Russia prepared to bolster Assad

Recent sightings of brand new Russian armoured vehicles in Syria, of types never previously supplied to its ally, suggest that with the Assad regime suffering serious reverses, Moscow is intent on redressing the military balance. On 20 August, a heavily-laden Alligator class landing ship of the Russian Navy, the Nikolay Filchenkov, was seen passing southwards through the Bosphorus.

On board, according to experts who have analysed the images, were trucks and armoured vehicles. The ship was believed to be on its way to Syria. Subsequently, the Syrian army has released video material that shows seemingly brand new BTR-82A infantry combat vehicles in action or on exercises - a variant of the vehicle that has never before been supplied to the Syrian military.

The vehicles appear to be in a Russian paint scheme and thus may have been taken straight from Russian army stocks. Separate images have emerged of Russian Tigre military utility vehicles; again a type that has not been exported to Syria before. Caution must always be used when analysing this kind of material.

But Joseph Dempsey, an expert at the International Institute for Strategic Studies in London, says that the images "if authentic, provide strong evidence of the BTR-82A and Tigr being in Syria". The delivery of these weapons raises all sorts of questions.

Syria did receive a small number of the related BTR-80 armoured personnel carrier in late 2013/early 2014 but the BTR-82A has a more modern and very different turret and weapons station.

Russia is one of the Syrian president's few foreign allies. It has long been a major arms supplier to Syria and, in the current crisis, it has given the Syrian regime important diplomatic support. Russia was instrumental in helping to negotiate the deal in 2013 under which the Assad regime gave up its chemical weapons.

Russia has long maintained a small naval base on the Syrian coast at Tartus. It represents a toehold for Russian influence in the region that peaked during the 1970s at the height of the Cold War. However, the Syrian crisis has alarmed Moscow. It is every bit as concerned by the rise of the murderous religious radicals of the so-called Islamic State (IS) movement as is the West.

Russia did not respond to the upheavals of the "Arab Spring" with the enthusiasm of many Western governments. And in retrospect, given that hopes for a democratic surge through the region have collapsed, Russia's hard-headed pragmatism looks to be a little more realistic than much of the West's "aspirational" diplomacy.

The Syria crisis also provides Russia with an opportunity. Its ties to the Assad regime make it a key player. Russian Foreign Minister Sergei Lavrov has forcefully reiterated Russia's position that the departure of Mr Assad cannot be a condition for any peace deal.

Such demands, he says, are "totally unrealistic and counterproductive". Russia insists that it is working to create what it calls a "broad anti-terrorist front" to counter IS. But the crucial thing for Russia is that the Assad regime must survive, whatever Mr Assad's personal fate in the longer term.

Much of the attention over recent weeks has focused on Russia's diplomatic efforts regarding Syria; its talks with senior Saudi and Iranian officials, for example. But, in the meantime, things have not been going well for Mr Assad on the ground, with his opponents pressing ever closer to the Alawite heartland - the coastal basin to the east of the Mediterranean, inland from Latakia and Tartus.

Amidst the uncertainty, a host of rumours are flying round of a much greater Russian role. Russia has denied that it recently delivered advanced warplanes to Syria. Some Israeli analysts, for example, believe that Russia is preparing to use its own aircraft against IS and might even be willing to play a greater role on the ground if the Assad regime's fortunes do not change.

This for now may be little more than speculation. The Russians themselves have denied that any aircraft have been deployed to Syria to prepare for strikes against IS. One expert, RuslanPukhov, a spokesman for Russia's arms industry, believes that what the Syrian forces require right now is "ammunition, light weapons, communications and UAVs [drones]".

Putin's support to Al Sisi

Between Feb. 9 and 10, Russia's President Vladimir Putin paid an official visit to Egypt, thus reciprocating an August 2014 Russia visit by Egyptian President Abdel Fattah al-Sisi. Shortly before Putin's trip, Moscow's analyst community suggested that the Russia-Egypt relationship might be elevated to a strategic partnership. The makings of such a shift included the parties' shared positions on a number of regional issues; closely aligned interests (particularly on fighting international terrorism); a successful track record of bilateral cooperation on various fronts; and a strong personal bond of trust between respective leaders.

Moscow took time to lean toward support for the Egyptian military, which had assumed power through an unprecedentedly large-scale manifestation of the popular will. However, the waiting game did not take long, as Russia's orientation toward support for Sisi in every possible way became obvious following Sisi's electoral victory. Already in 2014 trade and economic cooperation between the two nations developed at a brisk pace.

According to Egyptian Ambassador to Russia Mohammed al-Badri, who described Russia-Egypt ties as "picking up" across all areas of cooperation, last year's trade between the two countries stood at $3 billion. Meanwhile, Russia's Federal Customs Service cites an even higher figure of $4.6 billion between January and December, including $4.1 billion in Russian exports.

Notwithstanding certain misgivings about Egypt's security situation and an overall drop in the number of Russian nationals traveling abroad, more than 3 million Russians toured the country last year. In fact, Egypt's Tourism Minister HeshamZazua has gone as far as to propose that settlements with Russia in this sphere may be carried out in Russian rubles and Egyptian pounds, thus bypassing the dollar. Given Russia's sizable trade surplus, this does not appear implausible.

As Yuri Ushakov, an aide to the Russian president, told the press Feb. 5 that Egypt and the nations of the Eurasian Economic Community had agreed to set up a free trade area working group, and "a decision had been made to establish an appropriate research team that would examine this topic. Its first meeting will be held in Cairo in March or April this year."

As Putin told Egypt's Al-Ahram daily Feb. 8, *"We have established mutually beneficial and effective cooperation in the field of agriculture. Egypt is the major buyer of Russian wheat, Russia provides about 40% of grain consumed in that country; as for us, we import fruits and vegetables."* According to the president, Russia *"sees promising prospects in the field of high technology, particularly in the areas of nuclear energy, outer space use and sharing of Russia's GLONASS satellite navigation system."*

To Cairo, this continued rapprochement with Moscow is taking place against the background of a difficult relationship with Washington. Indeed, when Barack Obama's decision to invite Sisi to the White House was announced on July 14, 2014, Sisi excused himself and sent his prime minister instead, reminding observers of an interview he granted to Larry Weissman back in 2013. At the time, Sisi stated much more bluntly: *"The people of Egypt are aware of the fact that the USA has stabbed Egypt in the back with the Muslim Brotherhood and [Mohammed] Morsi. It is nothing that Egypt will easily forget, or forgive."*

On Oct. 24, 2014, the Russian website Inosmi quoted from an article titled *"Egypt gets ready for Putin's visit"* published in the UAE daily Al-Bayan, which said: *"As opposed to actions taken by Washington that considers a terrorist organization involved in pillage and looting as the lawful government and denounces its ouster as a coup, Russia is not ready to compromise, for it unabashedly calls a spade a spade."*

The Egyptian leadership was particularly peeved by the January 2015 tour of Washington taken by an Egyptian opposition delegation, including members of the Muslim Brotherhood's Freedom and Justice Party. They were received at the Department of State, according to political consultant Christof Lehmann.

Egypt's cooperation with Russia will, to a substantial degree, depend on whether Western nations continue to support Sisi financially. (Given the difficulties that Russia is facing on its own as a result of the sanctions and the oil price collapse, it is unlikely that it will shoulder the burden of pro bono assistance to Cairo.) Without the strong financial sustenance that Gulf countries such as Saudi Arabia, the United Arab Emirates and Kuwait provide to it, Egypt would be clearly unable to pay for Russian weaponry and military hardware imports, estimated by the media to total $3.5 billion last year already, including rotary and fixed-wing aircraft, as well as air defense systems.

It remains unclear what kind of aftershocks Egypt and the balance of power within the region at large would experience as a result of the "Saudi earthquake" that followed royal succession in the kingdom.

A vast field for cooperation has opened up for Cairo and Moscow, as each party has redoubled its efforts to mediate a settlement to the Syrian conflict. Prior to the advisory meeting of Syrian opposition, civil society and government representatives held in Moscow between Jan. 26-29 — the first meeting of its kind — opposition figures met in Cairo, even though no Syrian government delegation was there.

Still, the fight against international terrorism remains key to the political engagement of Moscow and Cairo. The Jan. 29 Sinai Peninsula attack against the Egyptian army by terrorists from the Wilayat Sinai organization (formerly known as Ansar Bayt al-Maqdis), which has pledged allegiance to the Islamic State, dealt a blow to Sisi. According to a February 2015 assessment by the Middle East Briefing, that attack "has increased the general sentiment in Egypt that the government of Sisi is unable to control the deteriorating security environment." In addition, Sisi accused the Muslim Brotherhood of conducting a campaign of terror.

Plus, the Egyptian authorities suspect that the terror attack was "aided by foreign special services." Tellingly, a Muslim Brotherhood communique issued on the attack day promised to "intensify the jihad" against the government, according to the Middle East Briefing. In this context, cooperation with Russia that, like Egypt, views the Brotherhood as a terrorist organization, receives a strong impetus.

Considering the dynamic evolution of its relations with non-Arab players such as Turkey, Israel and Iran, its ties to Egypt give Russia more clout as a Middle East player. Even though Moscow is both unable and unwilling to compete here with players wielding greater influence, primarily with Washington, it has not merely secured its niche but is clearly gaining ground.